A DIFFERENT
KIND
OF CLOSET

Mary Beth,

Thank you
so much!

A DIFFERENT KIND OF CLOSET

The Struggles
of Mental Illness

Roger L. Mohn

R·N·D

RND Publishing, Inc.

RND Publishing, Inc.
273 East Far Hills Drive
East Peoria, IL 61611
309-694-3021
roger@rndpublishing.com

Ordering Information:
Quantity sales. Special discounts are available on quantity purchases by corporations, associations, and others. For details, contact the publisher at the address above.
Orders by U.S. trade bookstores and wholesalers.
Please contact RND Publishing, Inc.
Tel: 309-694-3021 or visit www.rndpublishing.com.

Printed at Versa Press, Inc.
in the United States of America

Publisher's Cataloging-in-Publication data
Roger L Mohn: A Different Kind of Closet; The Struggle of Mental Illness
ISBN: 978-0-9961193-0-6
Library of Congress: 2016940792

First Printing March 2019

DEDICATED TO:

God: You created me. You know me. You are there for me; always. You give and take away. You have given me more than I deserve. I am amazed at Your continued work in my life and the paths You lead me on. Thank you!

My wife, Damara: *I owe you my life, literally.* You have been my rock, even though many times and for many years I didn't acknowledge just how much you meant to me. Your constant encouragement gave me the resolve to write this book, share my story, and help others understand the struggles of the mentally ill. You kept your faith that someday, somehow, this book and more would finally come out of me.

My parents, Rena and Kenneth (Toby) Mohn: Without them, I would have no story to share. R.I.P.

Our children, Christopher, Roger Jr., Elizabeth, and Chad: You know many of the stories I am about to share and lived many of them with me. I am so very proud of your courageous, adventurous, and independent spirits.

My brother and sister, Kenneth R. Mohn and Easter Dolan: You have the best stories; stories you experienced before I came along, and I thank you for the love you gave to me when I was young.

And finally, to the so-called "misfits" in life: You know who you are—the people who are just a little different than the rest, the dreamers, the thinking-outside-the-box people, the "boat-rockers,"—you think something must be wrong with you because you don't fit the norm. Let me tell you, had it not been for people like you, us, everyone would fit inside someone else's box, stamping out your creative brain juices until you become just like them or as they need you to be; programmed to perform, controlled into submission for their purposes—not really your dream, but helping them live theirs.

So many creative and talented people have had mental health issues and I honestly believe those who can recognize it, treat it, and harness it are the inventors, business entrepreneurs, singers; those who create their own destinies and refuse the status-quo in their lives. History has proven this with so many famous people who changed their world and the world around them through their creativity, talent, and tenacity. Now, I am not saying every talented, highly creative person has a mental illness; not at all. I am saying that many creative people do suffer with a mental illness, but they harness it, manage it, and even channel it to do some pretty great things. Yes, you are or can be the heroes of the world, the people who can get things done, despite yourself and your internal struggles. If you are one of those reading this, celebrate your differences! God didn't create you to be like everyone else. He molded you for His purpose, to challenge the so-called normal world. Keep in mind, Jesus didn't hang out with the "professional elite/status-quo" when He was on this earth. He befriended and hung out with many misfits, people who needed His help, love, encouragement, grace, healing, and most of all, forgiveness. Indeed, celebrate your unique personality, do not hide it! It's time!

ACKNOWLEDGMENTS

NAMI (National Alliance on Mental Illness): Thank you, NAMI, for opening a whole new world of understanding, hope, and healing for millions of people and families suffering in silence. You often are the only understanding hope of those people meeting together and knowing others who share this common bond. (www.nami.org)

Jason DeShaw: Jason, you are a huge inspiration to so many people! Your message of hope, healing, and recovery that you are sharing with others across the U.S. is phenomenal and you have been a huge inspiration to me in the short time I have known you.

Tahirah Ogletree: In the end, I think reading your book about surviving years of physical and mental abuse, then seeing the look on your face and knowing the joy in your heart watching your book come off the production line at Versa Press finally convinced me I needed to get my own book finished, printed, and out there. You are truly amazing! May God continue to bless you!

Cyndi Clark: I met Cyndi back in 2012 in Jackson, Mississippi, where she is a great graphic designer. She has helped many companies and people design book covers, layouts, and get their files ready for printing. She is awesome! Thank you, Cyndi, for all you do!

Laurie Parker: Wow! This lady has written over fifteen children's books and self-published five big novels! Laurie has such a great sense of humor, is filled with creative talent and just knowing her has inspired me so much. Laurie, you're amazing!

Versa Press, Inc.: Most of my adult life, I felt God directing me to write a book or books, about my life experiences growing up and dealing with mental illness around me, but a busy life, some inward self-doubt, and plain, old procrastination just got in the way. Those dreams, in the back of my head, just became a "someday when..." for me. My wife and family always encouraged me to write this book.

A few years back, God clobbered me hard—personally and financially—then amazingly and miraculously set my life on a different course. Ironically, I was given an opportunity at a new career in the book manufacturing business! I soon learned much more than the production side of the business. I also learned how to guide others through the process of getting their books into print. So now, it's my turn. I truly believe it was God's way of pushing me to do something He knew I could and would do with the right purpose and motivation. Sometimes God will pull the rug out from under you; get you out of your comfort zone, to show you His path for your life. This, for me, was exactly that.

Thank you, Bob Barth and Steve Kennell at Versa Press for your willingness to hire an uneducated, old supermarket owner like me and introduce me to a whole different world beyond grocery retail.

PREFACE

FIRST OFF, I am not a professional writer. That will probably be most evident as you read this book. I'm just a man who has lived an interesting life and a mental health advocate who wants to share his story with others who may have gone or are going through similar circumstances. No two people are the same, just as no two mental health issues are completely the same. Nor do each of us cope or deal with our problems the same. That's what makes us all unique. In the final edits of this book by an outside service, it was suggested to me that I tone down or remove much of the religious/faith comments as it may be offensive to those who do not believe in God, but I could not do that. My belief and faith in God are part of who I am and part of my story. To remove that about me, is to remove the essence of who I am, for it was my faith and belief in God that brought me this far. So, to those who do not believe in God, please read this book objectively for I cannot apologize for who I am.

Roger L. Mohn

I Have This Story...

I have this story inside of me that really must be told,
I need to put it into words before I get too damn old.

The pain, the love, the lessons of a life upon the edge,
Of insanity's pull in all directions, has become much like a
    wedge.

Stuck between the things I know and the man I wanted to be,
Stuck with indecision of the things that can literally set me free.

Tears fall down my checks when I recall the pain,
Of a life less remembered, a life so void and plain.

The guilt wells up inside of me as I can still hear her voice,
But I cannot block it out, for me there is no choice.

If life is but a season, I feel the slow pull of September,
I've wanted to draft this story, for as long as I can remember.

The past dances in my head, as reality soon fades away,
And takes me back to a place, never far from a street called
    Faraday.

CONTENTS

INTRODUCTION

MENTAL ILLNESS has become an important discussion today. Many people and families struggle in silence because the negative stigma surrounding mental illness is so great, they don't seek the help they need for the perceived shame that is associated with their illness. It's not just a, "Well, damn it! Stop feeling sorry for yourself and pull yourself together!" disease. It's far more than that. Mental illness will and does affect twenty percent of our world's population in one way or another. Whether it's bipolar disorder, schizophrenia, severe depression, borderline personality disorder, ADHD, OCD, etc., one out of five people are affected.

On top of that, mental illness is still not an "acceptable illness," meaning many people don't believe it's a real illness. They think it's just something that weak people or people with character flaws have, but nothing could be further from the truth. There is so much negative stigma surrounding mental illness that many people are afraid to open up about it and get the help they need.

If you are someone with mental health issues in your life or someone exposed to those with mental illness, I am sure you have your own wacky, weird, and surreal stories in which you can relate. You would know firsthand the struggle of mental illness and how you or those you know, cope with it.

The negativity of mental illness is permeated throughout our society because it is a very scary disease. Many who find themselves slipping from sanity don't know where to turn or are too scared because of the intense negative stigma surrounding mental illness and chose to battle it on their own, secretly, without medications or proper counseling.

I want to help erase the stigma surrounding mental illness by opening up my own family's story and my personal struggle in how I chose to deal with it for decades. So many people feel isolated and alone in this and I want them to realize that their struggle in silence only deepens the wounds for themselves and those around them. I was raised in what we now call a very dysfunctional home. My mother was diagnosed manic-depressive before I was born, so I only knew her in that way from the time I could remember until her death in 2008. I loved her very much, as I did my father, so what you read in this book is written in respect and love for them, though it may not seem this way as you read my story. But I firmly believe they did the best they could with what they had and what they knew to do in their lives.

My oldest son, Chad, has suffered with bipolar disorder since he was in his teens and I will share many stories of the constant ups and downs in his life and how we cope and work with that as a family.

Finally, I will share some of my own history with depression and how I continue to deal with that as well. It has been in my DNA, so I come by it honestly, and hope in sharing my stories those dealing with similar situations have hope that you or those you love can overcome and help others along the way. Please don't "suffer in silence." There is a lot of help out there, but you must come forward. Put away those feelings of negative stigma or shame and get help. I know that is not easy to do. There are so many great people out there that want to help, but we need you to make that first step; that acknowledgement that you need help. Once you do that, you will find the burden of that huge weight on you may not have been entirely lifted, but it is a big step in the right direction. Today's suicide rates are climbing, and I firmly believe the reason behind it is so many people are either scared to come forward or they think keeping it inside them, trying to overcome it alone, is the best way. It's not. Again, I say, please don't "suffer in silence."

As I enter into my 60s I have come to believe God has had his hand on my life the whole time, though I am very late in acknowledging this. I also believe I have spent my life in preparation for sharing this story with others and this is the right time for my family and me. Both my parents have long passed, and I can now share my stories without any pain to them. But to be fair, they would probably more than approve of my sharing these things with the world. They knew things weren't right in our family, but they did the best they could.

I have spent a large part of my life basically hiding our shame and living in much darkness about it. I don't want anyone else to do that. It's a tough road to go, both mentally and physically. So many people hide their lives "in the closet" due to public scrutiny of sharing their struggle. I am one of those people. For me, though, it is —

A different kind of closet.

"For I know the plans I have for you,"
declares the Lord, "plans to prosper
you and not to harm you,
plans to give you hope and a future."

Jeremiah 29:11 (NIV)

IT HAS TO START SOMEWHERE

I'M GOING to start with that great bible verse, Jeremiah 29:11, because any family and individual dealing with mental illness must have hope that the situation will get better or at least more stable than it has been. I want you, too, to be encouraged by that verse and really believe in it, no matter how hard that may be at the moment. As I unfold my personal story in this book, I am confident you will also see the parallels in your own stories, if you have a mental illness or it's in your family. One thing I have learned about this "secret club" of families who suffer in silence while dealing with their ill loved ones is the imposed shame that we all seem to share. This shame is, in part, thanks to the public and other's reaction and non-acceptance of mental illness as a true, legitimate illness.

Our family has dealt with mental illness for at least two generations, but I believe past generations have also experienced it, too. But back then there was no real name for it, other than melancholy depression, manic-depression, the blues, or catatonic withdrawal from life itself. It has only been in the last several decades that mental illnesses have seen truly defined names and terms such as bipolar 1, bipolar II, schizophrenia, and PTSD (Post Traumatic Stress Disorder).

I have known the sad ravages of mental illness my entire life. My mother was diagnosed manic-depressive, which today would be bipolar disorder. She remained crippled by the illness from well before my birth to her deathbed at age 84. When she was a teenager she was raped by her brother-in-law, became pregnant, and her family arranged a back-alley abortion. That was the beginning, the trigger, the catalyst that would create so much turmoil in her inner soul, that for the rest of her life she would struggle in and out of sanity.

When World War II ended, my father, like millions of other GI's, came home to start their lives again. I don't know the exact story of how they came together, but through the grace of God, somehow, they found each other and as they say, the rest is history...my history. They were married in 1945, right after the war, and in 1948 my brother, Ken, was born. Two years later, my sister, Easter, came along.

Here's how my own story unfolded:

It was 1956. In the post-war, baby boomer economy, two to four kids were about the norm, but since my father was struggling to earn a good living, I am sure two kids would have been just fine, but fortunately for me, it was not the end of the story.

My mother had still been severely depressed and manic during those years after my sibling's births. At one point, she was placed in the psychiatric unit at the old Illinois State Hospital in Bartonville, Illinois. Any time someone was sent to "Bartonville" in our area it was the same situation as "Bellevue" in New York State. Neither was a good place to be for anyone, but one of the only places that had any kind of help for the mentally ill.

Besides medication, what was the doctor's diagnosis for future recovery to keep her stable? He had told my father, "Toby, you need to have another baby to keep Rena occupied and focused." Now anyone who knows anything about true mental illness would tell you that adding another child to the equation is not the best idea or advice, but suffice to say, that was the solution that my father went for. Despite adding to my mother's illness, I truly thank God he did.

Years later my father would tell me that after my mom was pregnant, she had a relapse and had to go back into the state hospital while pregnant with me. That story always stuck in my head and up until the last few years, I haven't shared that with many people.

• • •

Those of us in this special "no casserole club" all have our own stories as to when we first realized ours was not one of the "normal" families in our neighborhoods. Far from it, our families always had some kind of high drama, catastrophic event or crisis going on, or if not, were about to.

Have you not heard of the "no casserole club?" Those of us involved in NAMI (National Alliance on Mental Illness) have used that quote many times and here's the explanation behind it: When someone in your family has some kind of a health crisis, be it a heart attack, kidney disease, surgery with home recovery, broken bones or myriad of other "socially accepted" illnesses, friends and relatives often stop by with food such as a hot casserole, deli tray, etc. When mental illness is diagnosed and there has been some kind of breakdown in the person involved, supportive visits by friends and family are usually nowhere to be found and those kinds of food or "casserole-to-recovery" gifts are non-existent. The personal visits shut down and the phone calls to "wish them well" pretty much shut down as well. Most people don't know what to say or do in this situation, so I am not passing judgement on them, just stating the facts as I know and have experienced. People are frightened by mental illness because it is such a mysterious disease and portrayed by the press and media in mostly horrific, negative fashions. So, you could ask, "Just how should I talk to them or approach them?" The exact same way you would for any other illness, since it is, in fact an illness of the brain. The families just want to know you're there for them and thinking of them. That's all.

Now in saying that, I want to also say that if you are truly a veteran of a family with mental illness, you also must have some kind of coping mechanism to keep yourself stable and grounded. For me, that was my twisted sense of humor. It was the only way I could really deal with what was happening around me. My mother was full blown manic-depressive and my father, God love him, found his coping mechanism in a beer bottle; several of them as needed for the occasion. I literally grew up in our local VFW (Veterans of Foreign Wars, Post 8662) hall and many taverns around the south end of Peoria, Illinois, back in the 60s. By the time I was 10, I think I knew every tavern location and bartender in the south end of Peoria.

I was able to compartmentalize my feelings in those trips to the taverns and having some place to enjoy myself other than our home and it helped me through, even though at that young age, I never fully realized it. Granted, it was not the best environment for a kid to grow up around, but it was my normal in a world that wasn't. It was years later that I came to understand just how much hanging out in those smoke-filled, drunken stupor, brawling places helped my sanity. Or that's my story and I am sticking to it. When you consider the alternative and the exposure to constant sadness, crying, wailing of my mother, and the arguments my mother and father would have as he came home drunk; my hanging out at the tavern, having fun, playing pool and enjoying all the Pepsi Cola and Blue Star potato chips a kid could indulge, it wasn't a bad alternative. Most times, it was the little old ladies and the guys that bought "little Roger" his fill of treats. I was a very skinny kid and looking back it was surprising that I wasn't overweight, but I would also ride my bike on many occasions to each of the taverns trying to hunt down my father to be with him, so those several miles-long bike trips in search of my father kept me in shape.

• • •

Neither of my parents went past the eighth grade in school. My mother's parents farmed her and her seven siblings out to local farm families and the kids never saw a dime of that money, as it went to keep their family fed, clothed, and sheltered. That was a normal thing back in the depression era for poor families with no education or other skills, to earn a better living. My father went to work in coal mines in the area, as did his father before him. It was just the way it was back on Dutch Hill in old south-town Peoria during the early 1930s depression years.

My father, despite his affection for alcohol and coming home drunk many nights of the week, managed to pull himself up each morning and go to work, putting in his full eight hours. I never knew him to call in sick or miss work. I was always amazed at that. He worked in a foundry and came home every night reeking of that smell with dirty clothes and face. He owned our (mortgaged) home, kept food on the table, and clothes on our back, and for that, I am eternally grateful. In some weird way, I think watching that—his commitment to getting himself to work every day when the night before was rough—helped instill a great work ethic in my siblings and me. No matter what, we go to work unless our arms or legs have been sawed off or we're incapacitated in some other way.

We never suffered any physical abuse, as neither of my parents was physically abusive toward each other either. The abuse in our family came from neglect. Had DCFS (Department of Children and Family Services) been around in our neighborhood, the chances would have been high that we may have ended up in foster homes. My brother, sister, and I talk jokingly about that sometimes, but the reality of the situation would have been no joke at the time. Most times, we could stay out as late as wanted, go wherever we felt brave enough to, and use our own judgment in that. It really was amazing that we didn't fall prey to the nightmares that haunt many parents. More than amazing, it was a miracle given our circumstances.

Since my brother and sister, Ken and Easter, are eight and six years older than me, respectively, I always say they have the best stories, because being just two years apart, they got to experience my mother's manic-depressiveness as a team. Whereas, by the time I could remember things, they were older and I wasn't part of their everyday life.

It's kind of the way it is in families dealing with mental illness. We all have these stories, some good, and some bad in our past. Sometimes we come forward to share them with someone who has a similar experience, but many times we keep the stories hidden inside us, filling ourselves with shame because our families weren't like TV's *Ozzie and Harriet* family or our parents weren't Ward and June Cleaver, Cliff and Clair Huxtable, or Carl and Harriett Winslow. Those great, more than perfect TV parents who always seemed to know what was right for their TV families. I always knew my parents were not the norm when I engaged with other kids and their parents. I did envy so many kids in my neighborhood and had always dreamed of what my life would be like if I just had parents like those. Rena and Toby Mohn were more like the TV show *All in the Family*'s Edith and Archie Bunker. My mother wore those loose, printed house dresses like Edith, had Edith's shrill toned voice, and my father's mannerisms and beliefs were right in line with Archie's. My mother's voice was a cross between Edith Bunker and Marge Simpson. Seriously, they were as close to Edith and Archie as you could get, and it is a lot of fun now looking back at our family situations knowing we pretty much came out of it OK, along with the help and influence of other families, friends, and relatives, were we got to witness a normal family dynamic in action. Each of us at least got to hang around normal families who rubbed off on us a bit. I can't speak for my siblings, but for me, there were so many times that I longed for what other kids had; that normal, undramatic, ho-hum, cookie-cutter, All-American, play-by-the-rules handed-down-through-the-ages, normal family.

It was never to be, of course, and as I realize, God has a plan for everyone, out of every situation, to use that experience, pain and/or suffering for good if you can firmly believe that and find a way to make it so. Life at 1610 Faraday wasn't the worst a kid could go through, not by a long shot, and I look back at so many things in my life and realize I didn't have it as bad as many other people that I would meet later in life. Even in all that, God had blessed me and had a plan for the rest of my life. I just didn't know or even appreciate how my life would go.

YOU KNOW I MUST SHARE...
SOME QUICK SIBLING STORIES

NOW, WITH the fact that Ken and Easter were much older than me, when I was just a toddler, they got to experience mom's full-blown manic states and they have so many memories of her doing and allowing so many things that most kids will never get to experience. This is the way it is in homes with mental illness. We all have this common bond of background stories that only families with mental illness in them can or would appreciate. Perhaps appreciate is not the correct word, because at the time it happens, no one would think about appreciating anything about it, but as time goes on and you look back at those things and experiences, you do learn to appreciate the fact that you made it through and hopefully, made it through OK. I know many people don't get through it unscathed, and for that, I am so sorry for them. With my siblings and me, we put on an "armor plate of humor" that got us through many dark days but also a lot of *fun times with mom*.

One of the best stories Ken and Easter shared with me was once when they wanted to color with crayons and apparently do it on a large scale on the living room wall. So, my mom pulled out the living room sofa and encouraged them to let out their inner Van Gogh. Seriously. But then what about my father? What would he do when he got home and saw what they did and what his wife allowed? No worries. My mom told Ken and Easter they could only color below where the sofa lined up with the wall; if he couldn't see it they couldn't get in trouble.

Or there was the time during a very cold winter, they wanted to ice skate outdoors, but we didn't live near a lake or pond. Again, mom to the rescue! She decided to open the garage door and turn a water hose loose on the floor. Soon a very nice skating rink appeared. I never heard what happened when dad got home on that one, but these kinds of stories were typical in our home growing up with Rena.

A lot of times when we got together, we would discuss how we raised ourselves like a pack of wolves, and that wasn't far from the truth. There were many times mom was in the state hospital, a local hospital's psych ward, or the Zeller Zone Mental Health Facility in Peoria for mental illness. She just wasn't around many times in our lives.

• • •

Mom knew when she was slipping and at those times she would tell my dad, *"Tob! It's time to lock me up again!"* He'd drive her to either the psych ward at St. Francis Hospital or to Zeller's for a few weeks stay at CLUB MED—she was being heavily medicated and sedated. They would either induce electro-shock therapy or use heavy doses of lithium to calm her. I remember visiting her after the shock treatments; she would be in this zombie-like state. She knew who I was, but speech and communicating was hard. It was like she was hypnotized in some kind of trance.

When the movie, *One Flew Over the Cuckoo's Nest* came out in the 70's, I was already well educated on what that situation was like in real life. So many of the patients on her ward had the same mannerisms and characteristics of those depicted in the movie. The movie was about as close to being in a real ward as I am sure Hollywood could get and I really could relate to that movie. We had to take care of ourselves and there were a lot of things that weren't right in that situation, but we did the best we could. Occasionally a relative might help, but most often what we heard from the relatives was not support, but comments like, *"You poor kids! You shouldn't have to grow up with a crazy mother!"* It was like a little stab-in-the-heart when I heard those things and I would either be silent or shrug it off, but deep inside it was a real, cutting wound that added to my growing shame of the whole situation.

It was all we knew though. For us, it was the norm. Yes, not right, of course, but we didn't know how bad it was, we just existed in it and grew through it. That's the way it is in all families with mental illness. You know it's not right. You know it's not the way it's supposed to be, but it is the hand you're dealt, so you do your best to play that hand and survive it. We often joke that we were so lucky that none of us three ended up as an alcoholic, drug abuser, or criminal. It was more of God's miracle in our lives than not.

• • •

If you believe, God will use every situation, every bad or good thing in our lives for His glory, but in His time. It has taken over five decades for me to understand and realize the purpose of what I went through, to share with you, is God's purpose for the latter part of my life. I just wasn't ready yet to bring this all to the surface, reliving many memories and reliving that shame I had. The shame for me in my youth was that my parents were less than normal. The shame I have now, as an older adult, is that I didn't have more respect and compassion for them, realizing that it was the very best they could do with who they were and how they were raised. I continue to ask God's forgiveness for this and I know that my forgiveness has been paid on the Cross.

I don't know how many times when I was a kid, that I would watch my friends and their families do normal things like go on picnics together, go out to dinner, take family vacations, or just go for a nice drive in the country. I had never experienced any of that, really, until I had my own children. When I did get that opportunity, I more than enjoyed doing those things as a family and I think I even tried to overdo it as a makeup for my lost youth. My children have been many places and seen many things around the country with us, together as a family, places I could have only dreamed about when I was kid.

Ken and Easter have so many stories I could probably do another book just on theirs and someday hope to. Without a whole lot of great guidance and discipline in the house, weird things would happen. Like the time Ken said he would pay Easter to hang and drop out of a second story window for one dollar. She did, and dropped, unhurt, and of course, Ken refused to pay up because he never had the money in the first place. You know, kid's stuff! He would tear the heads off her dolls and throw them out the window for the dogs in the yard to use as chew toys. You know; more kid's stuff!

Once they went out in the woods, built a fire, and then stretched a rubber inner tube over the fire, as a dare or bet to see who would hold on the longest before it snapped. Now keep in mind, they were probably eight or ten years old at the time. The tube caught fire, snapped in two and covered Easter's arms in hot rubber burns. When I think of that one, I'm glad I was too young to have been a part of that.

Another story I like to share is my *Ice Cream Story*. In the early 60s in mid America, just about every other street corner in the city had a family grocery store on it. My dad would leave just enough money with mom to buy the food for our dinner that night when he got home. Mom always liked to please her children, to an extreme fault, due to her nature and illness. If the Mr. Softee Ice Cream truck happened through our neighborhood on a hot summer day, mom would use dad's grocery money to buy ice cream and treats for the neighborhood kids! She just couldn't help herself. When dad got home, we had no dinner, but they would throw whatever we had in the cupboards together to feed us. Many times, our dinner consisted of a gallon of milk with canned tomatoes mashed up and it became tomato soup. I know, gross, but it was all we had in those times. I can't stand tomato soup today because of it and haven't had a bowl of it since I was a kid.

• • •

These are all stories, trust me, that many children with a parent with mental illness can tell. The boundaries of right and wrong get stretched a lot in homes with mental illness. The stories would be different, perhaps better or worse, but we all share that same common bond of going through it and hopefully surviving it. When I meet someone with a similar background, and believe me they are out there, these kinds of stories always come up and we then share how we coped and got through it. I am always amazed how many people tell me it was their warped sense of humor that got them through. It was how I got through it and I am greatly appreciative of that. I think it was God's way of telling me, *This too, will pass"* but I never knew the how or why of it all until I grew much older.

Mom just had a hard time saying no to anything. On rainy days, I could ride my bike in the house if I wanted—as best I could of course—banging the walls, the furniture, the cats, it didn't matter as long as I was happy. My mom would smile and watch me go, back and forth from the kitchen to living room and back again, over and over. Our house was a very small frame, tract home with just two upstairs bedrooms in the south end of Peoria. You had to walk through one bedroom to get to the back bedroom. The front bedroom was partitioned off with a hanging white sheet, with my parents' bed in the front of the room and my sister's in the back. Ken and I had the other bedroom but shared the same bed. There was only one bathroom in the house off the kitchen, a living room, and a dining room. That was it on a small city lot. A small wooden frame house at 1610 Faraday in the heart of the south end of Peoria, where it still stands today, now occupied by my brother and his wife, as he wants to finish his years in the home he grew up in. Ken has remodeled that house into the best on the block, whereas when we were growing up, it was just about the worst on our block.

LIFE WITH RENA

LIFE WITH Rena was a journey. One summer day, she was hanging clothes on an outdoor clothesline in our backyard. A washer and dryer were a luxury we could not afford. I was upstairs in a bedroom and suddenly I heard her scream frantically at the top of her lungs, *"I want to die! I want to die! Somebody please listen to me! I want to die!"* She kept screaming this over and over again as she was hanging those clothes on the line. It seemed like forever. As I looked out the window, a crowd of neighbors gathered around her trying in futility to calm her down. I was around seven or eight years old at the time and home alone with her. I panicked and then found myself trying to hide from view. I crept down against the wall in between a cedar hope chest and the corner. I found myself staring at the black rotary phone that sat on that hope chest, yet I was too scared to call for help. Her screaming persisted. I looked out long enough to see two or three police cars now on the scene. Yet, I still hid. Soon, I could hear footsteps coming up the stairs. The stairs were just painted wood and the echo of footsteps resonating in the small, steep stairwell made it sound like an army coming up those stairs. Still I hid. As the footsteps reached the top of the stairs, I was scared out of my wits thinking maybe they were going to take my mother to jail this time.

The next thing I know, it was a police officer and a neighbor lady who found me. I wasn't crying; I was just scared to death. That's all, just scared. I had seen my mother's mood swings, just never so severe and never before by myself. Looking back, I think it was a turning point for me. Maybe it was at that point that I realized our family really was different. We had something wrong in our family. The police were able to call my father and he came home from work. It was the beginning of yet another cycle. She would spend several weeks at Zeller Zone. I would visit her many, many times on these occasions. I would get to witness the other patients or inmates as I would think of them in my mind. My mother always seemed to be the sanest of them all.

• • •

When I get comfortable enough to share my stories with people, those who know me now are often taken aback or in complete dismay that these things could have happened in my life and that we got through childhood and into adults unscathed. Now, that's an interesting word, unscathed. I don't believe Ken, Easter, or I did make it out totally unscathed, but we did make it out. Each of us has our own quirky things about us, be it my brother and sister's OCD or my warped sense of humor, compiled with a giant dose of major depression every now and again. You don't go through anything like that unaffected; it's just how much did it affect us? None of us are alcoholics, drug users, or skid row bums, so for that, I am grateful. We have each been overall successful in our own right of what we have chosen to do with our lives.

Now granted, these kinds of things can happen even in great, highly educated, wealthy families because mental illness is an equal opportunity disease and affects one out of five people at some time in their lives, be it with bipolar disorder, schizophrenia, depression, OCD, ADHD, and so much more. I want to share my life and stories for those that have gone through these things but are afraid or ashamed to talk about it because I used to feel that way, big time, but no more. I now enjoy sharing our family's craziness in the hopes that it will pull others out of their own, self-imposed closet of shame and when you do that, you can begin the healing and understanding process.

With my mother, you just never knew what she'd say or do next. Each day was a new experience, one that either filled me with laughter, with shame, or both. As a boy, I didn't really understand or fully appreciate the way she could verbalize what she wanted to express. Being the youngest child in the family I was probably, no, I was a little spoiled. So much so, that if any of my own children did what I am about to tell you,

I'd have probably punished them severely. But with Rena, you could get away with just about anything.

She kept me nursing a bottle until I was five years old and in kindergarten. Seriously, she did. In fact, when my little friends, local neighborhood kids came over, she'd give them all bottles and there we were, all lying on a couch or in chairs watching Captain Kangaroo on TV, all sucking away on bottles. One day, my brother came home from school, saw this, and blew his top. He grabbed all the bottles from our mouths, went to the kitchen, and cut the bottles in half, throwing them in to the garbage. My mom wailed and wailed over that, yelling at him, but no matter, he knew he did the right thing. Of course, my friends all took off for home when this action started. I didn't know any better and sometimes she'd put chocolate milk in the bottles if we had any in the house. It's just so strange to think about, looking back at it all.

One morning she'd been crying while lying in bed, as she did so many times. You could hear her all hours of the day or night sobbing in her bed. She would go through crying cycles, too. For what seemed months upon end, she would lay in bed sobbing. Other times, she'd just sleep. I think a good portion of my childhood was spent just watching her sleep the day away. If she wasn't in a psychiatric ward somewhere, she'd be home in bed. In that old two-story, frame house with a coal furnace, no air conditioning, and with absolutely no heating ductwork to the upstairs—the only thing we had for heat was a small 12 inch by 12 inch floor register cut into the middle of one bedroom, directly over the dining room below—you prayed for the heat to rise through it during the winter months, but still, mom slept.

It was also, oddly enough, our window into mom and

dad's bedroom directly below us. As we grew a little older and Easter wanted her privacy as a young girl, dad converted the dining room into their bedroom. Easter had the room right at the top of the stairs and Ken and I had the one in the front of the house. As I said before, there was no hallway, so you had to walk through Easter's room to get to ours. Each room had just one light bulb hanging from the ceiling, which you turned on by pulling the chain attached to the fixture. That was it. Nothing special, but it was home. It was primitive, with poverty written all over it by today's standards.

In looking through that 12-by-12 register in the floor, down into their bedroom, we didn't watch them having sex, as I can never remember that, but we did watch them talk, argue, or listen to her softly crying in that bed. It was like a small window into their lives as a husband, wife, father and mother. I would spend hours looking through that hole in the floor at their world below. I also loved listening to them both saying the Lord's Prayer each night as they lay there.

THIS CHICKEN DIED FOR YOU!

MOM WOULD cook me breakfast sometimes, mainly eggs and toast before school. I was lucky in that respect. I think I was maybe seven or eight at the time. On this morning, she was in bed crying but asked me if I had wanted something to eat. I told her I did, and she got up looking so depressed, so lonely, so tired, her hair matted down from hours of unrest, yet she did get up because of wanting to give me breakfast. She was going to cook two eggs and some toast.

I liked my eggs sunny-side up, unbroken yokes on the plate.

As she cooked each egg, somehow, she managed to break open the yokes as she placed them on the plate. Being the unappreciative brat I was, I refused to eat them broken like that. Now, right now, right here, most mothers would have said, *"You'll eat the eggs regardless if the yokes broke!"* Not Rena. She continued cooking eggs, over and over until she finally got them right for me. It was a ritual we went through every time she attempted to cook those eggs. During this process, this day, she began to cry. I didn't know what to do, but I sure didn't care for those broken, runny eggs. She looked at me, with so much sadness in her eyes, her voice in this monotone quiver of a whisper and said, *"Roger, Roger, this chicken died for you! Do you know that? This chicken died so that you can eat."* She had so much sadness and seriousness in her face as she said it and with that voice that I felt so guilty and bad for making her cook so many eggs. It was just another Rena moment, but one that had lasting memories for me to this day. I really don't remember ever letting her cook me eggs after that.

It was those kinds of moments and memories that I still think about each day with her. She could say things that no one would ever even think about, let alone say. It wasn't done in spite or in meanness; it was done from total innocence and ignorance.

• • •

One time, I had to take a bus ride with her. Since she never had a driver's license in her life, she never drove a car, never had a desire to get behind a steering wheel. She relied upon dad and relatives to take her places. One day, she had an eye doctor appointment, and no one was available to drive her. Dad told her she'd have to take the bus, since there was a bus stop at the end of our block. This is the only time I ever remember going anywhere with her alone on a bus. It was a ride I'll never forget.

Before I share this memory, I want to insert a disclaimer here. You will soon read the dreaded "N" word in describing an African-American man. Yes, I could totally leave that out, but I am putting it in exactly how I heard and experienced it because it is important to know what I went through. Please, I am not prejudiced, a bigot, or any of a myriad of labels one likes to use when someone uses the "N" word. I was beat up and bullied in junior high and high school, severely, by people of color, so if anyone should be racist, I should be, but I carry no malice toward anyone, as I know many of my white friends were not kind at all toward many black people at school when I went there and it was an equal, mutual feeling from the blacks. I did grow up in a prejudiced home in a white, but very poor neighborhood. I am so thankful that I did not grow up in the south when segregation was everywhere. I couldn't even imagine seeing a White Only sign on a drinking fountain, lunch counter, or in public anywhere. For me, it's just hard to picture in my head. As I have said, my father, who I love and respected very much, was like Archie Bunker in real life. My children did not grow up in a prejudiced home, I am very proud to say. It was a different era then and an ignorant one, I want to add. I subscribe to Martin Luther King Jr.'s famous saying, in that I judge a person by the content of their character, not the color of their skin. Dr. King was a courageous, brilliant, and peaceful man. He definitely deserves the recognition for his civil rights work and changing our country and the world for the better.

As we boarded the bus, she paid the fare and found us seats

in the middle of the bus. Sitting in the back of that bus, there was an old black man. There were just a few others on that bus besides us, but he was the only black person on the bus. Being a poor, young white boy from a white section of town at the time, I didn't have much experience meeting or even seeing black people. For us, it was a rarity in South Peoria in the early 1960s. Whether my mother noticed me looking at the man or not, I'll never know, but I do remember what she said to me in another one of those simple, politically incorrect, ignorant ways. She leans into me with this soft voice of a whisper and says, *"Roger. Look at that poor, old nigger man back there. Isn't that awful? That poor old Chocolate Drop!"* She would call black people "Chocolate Drops" all the time. Of course, I didn't have a clue about what was coming next out of her mouth. If that wasn't bad enough, then she drops the bomb on me! In that same sheepish whisper, with this look of pity on her face, perhaps a glint of a smile, she says, *"Roger, isn't that just a shame? That poor man gets up every morning, looks in the mirror, and sees an old black nigger face staring back at him! No matter how hard he tries to wash it off, it's never coming off. Wouldn't that be just awful, Roger, to look at that in the mirror every day? That poor, old nigger man!"*

Yes, the "N" word is horrible, but back then it was part of so many people's vocabulary, so very wrong, yes; but nonetheless it was. I debated hard whether to include that in this book, but I just felt I had to, from the standpoint of fully understanding the kinds of things I heard and experienced in my childhood. Things that are wrong to say to a child, teach a child, but things that were part of her personality. I just remember, besides being in shock, laughing to myself, despite it not being a funny issue, and trying to keep it all in without this man finding out about what she just said. I could tell he was looking at us and I don't believe he'd heard her; otherwise there might have been trouble. I also remember that I couldn't wait to get off that bus. Now, she said this not in a hurtful way to me, but from the innocent ignorance of her own background. She didn't stop to think about how it would affect me. Those things were not part of her thought process. If she wanted to say something she did.

Again, I was old enough to remember this, but still perhaps, too young maybe to even comprehend anything like racism, prejudice, or even ignorance of the subject at that age. I just remember it as being another one of those strange, weird, but often funny things that came out of her mouth when I was kid. As I look back at that day, in that bus, I probably learned even more about my mother's illness, even if I didn't realize at the time. Life with her was an adventurous journey in never knowing what would happen next. Would she breakdown again and be committed to another hospital? Would she say something we'd regret later in conversations? You just never knew.

A few years would go by and she would get a little better and a little worse at times. In her depressed state of mind, she threatened suicide to us about every day at this point.

• • •

A typical story from my past would be my mother standing at the top of the stairs, a long butcher knife in her hand, peering through the chain-locked bedroom door saying, *"Roger! Roger! I am going to kill myself! I want to die! I want to die! Watch me, Roger! Here I go!"* I would watch in fear and horror as she would make the motions with that butcher knife to her throat or her wrists like she was about to do it. We kept the door chained because this same scene would go on and on for many days at a time. She'd walk up those steps and go through that routine over and over. So much so, that eventually my sister and I would say, *"Just do it, mom! Go ahead! You keep threatening! Why don't you just do it?"* We would be so cruel in saying this. Her reaction would be to scream it louder and louder, over and over again. She would eventually retreat down the stairs for a while, things would get silent and then she would head back up the stairs for another round or two. Many times, she'd even tell us, *"I'm putting newspapers on the floor, so the blood doesn't go everywhere."* Like we even thought or cared about the mess it was going make over her actually doing it? This would go on many, many times during my childhood and well into my adult life with her. We would just accept it, not thinking about what it might be doing to us long term. It was our way of surviving it all.

I was always really good about keeping it together, keeping it hidden, every time she'd say, *"Roger, I'm having a nervous breakdown! It's time to lock me up again!"* And then she would cry frantically in that wailing voice, crying over and over, *"I'm no good, Roger, I'm just no good! I want to die, Roger!"* It was at those points guilt would surface in me because then I'd want her locked up too, as her torment was ours as well. I know it wasn't right, but it was another way of coping, dealing with that pain inside me. I carried shame and embarrassment with me my whole life because of how I grew up, the constant battle of her sanity and the constant battle I had within myself because of it. The neighbors were cruel and brutal against us. It was like we were some kind of criminal low-life, sub-human family.

There were so many embarrassing moments with mom; it's hard to recall them all. Once, when mom was introduced to a very stocky woman and I use that phrase lightly, mom's comment to her was, *"Wow! You sure must like to eat!"* I remember it well as I sank inside myself and wanted just to crawl away, slither perhaps, like a snake into a bush.

Another time, my brother took mom and dad out to dinner at a very nice restaurant, Jumer's Castle Lodge, in Peoria. This place has long since closed, but in its heyday, it was a nice place near the south end of Peoria. This restaurant was known for its great food and especially its old-world German atmosphere. There was an area in the restaurant called The Library, with antique bookshelves, a medieval look to it all, with plush high-back chairs. As the waiter came around asking how everything was, he asked my mother, *"Mrs. Mohn, how is your fish?"* My mom bluntly replied in her loud Edith Bunker voice, *"It tastes like shit!"* The waiter was in shock and my brother then explained that she didn't eat much fish and smoothed over the situation, but he and my sister-in-law, Pam, knew it was just my mom's way of saying she didn't like it, whether anyone liked it or not. It wasn't done from malicious meanness; it was done from not being out in public enough, being very uneducated and unable to control her thoughts versus her spoken words.

We now call it *Growing up Rena* and look back with amazement. No one died, no one was murdered in our home, no one committed heinous crimes against anyone or the public, we never witnessed anything like that in our lives, so it was just the way it was and as I say now, compared to many other dysfunctional households where those kinds of things had occurred, we were lucky.

THE THOUGHT PROCESS

As you have by now surmised, people with mental illnesses don't exactly think the same as those without that affliction. I don't mean this in a negative, demeaning way. People with mental illness want to be part of a normal life, but it can be a daily struggle to keep it all together. It's just a fact, as they live with something that most people don't, a brain disease, which causes their normal thought processes to go astray at times. Many days, they must think in terms of just getting through each hour of the day without an episode, hoping at least to get something productive done. Internal pep talks are a must and many times, it is the only way they make it through the day. Those who have never experienced mental illness, from their perspective think anyone with mental illness needs to just pull themselves together and stop the pity-party.

If only it were that easy. People with mental illnesses think that too, but they can't. It is a true brain disease and the issue is not that they don't want to, it's just the process is so hard many give up and stay in their world of sadness, depression, and hopelessness. The best chance they have is to get on the right medications and then STAY ON THE MEDS! I often tell my son, *"If you had a heart condition or a liver condition and your doctor said if you didn't take the meds, you could die; then of course, you would stay on those meds, right? Well the same is true with mental illness."* The meds are what helps keep you stable, productive, and feeling good. But, in the mind of a person with mental illness, the stigma that surrounds mental illness is so negatively intense that many people look at the meds as a temporary crutch to just get by until they feel better and they do not realize the long-term commitment they must make to stay mentally healthy.

The most common problem among those with mental illness is when they feel better they then feel they don't need the meds and stop taking them. Then the cycle starts all over again. They relapse, often hospitalized or worse, then are forced to get back on the meds when if they had stayed on them in the first place, things would be so much better.

I call this, sadly, the cycle of insanity, meaning doing the same thing over and over, yet expecting improved or different results is, by definition, insanity. It's a harsh word in the mental illness community, but so true nonetheless. People with mental illnesses just can't pull themselves together. It just doesn't work that easy. The successful people with mental illness are those that have recognized and accepted it is a lifelong illness and they must commit to the meds as well as seeking help when they do feel any kind of an episode coming on, be it depression, mania, anxiety, etc.

The late actress, Patty Duke, was one who recognized this and stayed on the meds. My wife and I had the opportunity to meet her at a speaking event in Rockford, Illinois, many years ago. She was a very gracious and caring person, so willing to share her story with the world. In her talk and to us afterwards, she told us lithium was her wonder drug and it was the most helpful of any medications she was on. Lithium is often looked at as a pioneer, old school drug, but it still helps millions of people and it worked for Patty.

• • •

We can always tell when our son has not been taking his meds. He's agitated, anxious, or depressed. He'll call us on the phone several times a day to talk to us about the same things, over and over again. We can tell him that we just discussed it, but it doesn't matter, he'll keep calling. You get to the point, of course, that you don't want to answer his phone call, but then again, what if he is in some real trouble this time or it is a true emergency? Such is life in the family of the mentally ill. It's a lifelong situation, but you realize in your special way and situation that other people and families have it so much harder than you and that is not only a comfort to get you through it, but it is so very true indeed. So, you ask God for the guidance, strength, and perseverance to make it through yet another day.

Years ago, in a weekend training seminar for NAMI's Family-to-Family class teachers, I heard so many stories in the room that made mine pale in comparison. I was only one of two guys in the room comprised of mainly women for training. As each of us explained how we got involved in NAMI and then shared our own personal stories, I heard so many sad stories and it made our family's situation look very good in comparison. One lady said her son never had any problems whatsoever and he had just graduated with honors from a renowned chiropractic college. He was given the task, which he accepted gladly, of organizing the graduation party. Without notice and warning he just crashed into a mental mess and from that point forward he was in and out of mental hospitals. He eventually found stability but still had the occasional bouts with the illness and had to work hard to stay stable. No one knows why; it just happened. That's exactly what mental illness can do, come on without a lot of warning signs. Something just triggers it.

Another woman shared her story of coming home to find that every wall and window in her home had been punched out and broken with a baseball bat that her son was holding in his hands when she walked through the door of her home that night. Afraid and shocked, but keeping a cool head about her, as we all learn to do in dealing with mental illness, she suggested that he take a hot bath and calm down. He agreed and while in the bathtub she had to call the police to come intervene in the situation. It was a very sad story and she broke down in tears while telling it, as many of the others did in their stories. It just rips your heart out knowing the things that families dealing with mental illness go through. Our son rarely had fits of absolute rage, the anger is in him, but contained. I give him credit for keeping that in check, despite his other highly erratic behavior from time to time. We believe now that he would never hurt anyone else, only himself.

Yet another mom told the story of her honor roll son going into severe panic attacks because he believed the government had planted a camera in his head and was recording his every thought and movement. The stories were incredible, but each person in that room was bound and determined to make a difference not in just their lives via NAMI's Family-to-Family program, but in many others, they would soon go on to help. None of us volunteered to be in the family of mental illness, but now that we are, after many years of trying to cope and overcome the situation we finally realized that we were not alone in all of this. So many others, millions, across the U.S. and world are dealing with the exact same things. Each of our stories is different, perhaps, but the issue is still the same: we live with the fact that mental illness affects us and our families.

These are the sad stories. On the flip side, most people with mental illnesses are extremely smart and talented. No? Hollywood, our government, and the media are filled with people who have mental illnesses who have found ways to either overcome or keep their illness in check via the right meds, counselors, therapists, etc. There is a huge list of these celebrities who have proudly gone on to do very great things despite setbacks. Just Google *celebrities with mental illness* and you'll find tons of them, both living and passed, who have dealt with some type of mental illness in their lifetime. Abraham Lincoln, our 16th President, was one. He suffered much depression over the years. And let's then consider Mary Todd, his beloved wife. She spent time locked away in a mental institution after his assassination, but truth be told, she could have easily been institutionalized during his presidency. The story is fascinating. These people are the true champions of mental illness whether they want to be known that way or not.

• • •

No one signs up for mental illness, just as no one signs up for cancer, heart disease, kidney disease, or other illness. It just happens. Like other physical diseases, mental illness is considered highly genetic and can be handed down, generation to generation. One famous family that comes to mind is the Hemingway family. The famous author, Ernest Hemmingway's father took his own life, as did Ernest at the age of 61 and finally his daughter, Margaux followed. If you want to see a great documentary by Margaux's sister, Mariel, rent or buy *Running from Crazy*. It is an in-depth look into their lives and I am sure anyone with a history of mental illness in their family will easily relate to the stories in the film. It tells their story in detail.

A more recent celebrity whose family has dealt with mental illness is the actress Glenn Close. Her sister has bipolar disorder and Glenn has been very involved in helping to reduce the stigma of mental illness, forming an incredible foundation to raise awareness and money to help others. That organization's website is www.bringchange2mind.org. Like NAMI's, it's a great website and an awesome resource.

I used to watch my mother go in and out of her episodes and I always thought, *"Why can't you just pull yourself together and act right?"* You only needed to say that to her once and the tears would flow as she would break down yet again in full blown depression and then I felt like crap for even bringing it up, even though it was out of sheer frustration. My friends would laugh at her and instead of defending her, I cowered into myself in depression over the whole situation.

I have fought depression, off and on, much of my life as well, as I tried to deal with the whole thought process. I have watched my mother, when I was child, walk outdoors on a frozen winter day with no shoes on her feet, to pick up frozen dog turds from our yard as neighbors would look on in wonder. If I left as much as a pencil at home, she would walk to my school in the pouring rain or a snowstorm to bring me that single pencil. Once, when I was in the first or second grade, she didn't think I had washed my face before school, so she walked to my school, several blocks away, wet washcloth in hand and wiped my face in front of the whole class. Why would she do these things? That was my mother. She thought these things were perfectly fine and she was doing the right thing, even though the reality of it was totally bizarre behavior. Then I was ashamed, but now I wear those stories and experiences as badges of honor for I believe this is what God wishes me to do with the remainder of my life and it is time to share my story with so many others. I hope to bring people out of their shame, out of their secret closet of hidden memories, and let them know it's OK. You made it through and God has a reason for your life too.

• • •

Let's talk about God for a minute. Whether you believe, or you don't, is your choice of course. I always believed, but I fully admit there were times in my life that God was on the back burner and I placed Him there because I just didn't realize His importance or calling. I was young, dumb, ignorant, and arrogant. As I got older, I came to realize the "why" of everything I have gone through and it was for His purpose, that when the time was right, I would come forward with boldness and share my story with His strength to do so. I am there now. I will talk more about this later, but I am here today because of God's grace and mercy in my life. If you don't know God or if you don't believe in Him, I pray as you read this book, you reconsider and hopefully you too, will find that gentle calling of Him and His son, Jesus, within you. I love it when people say they found God, but the reality is God was always there with them, they just came to realization of that and found new peace and purpose with Him because of it. I was one of those people. People expect that if they are to hear or be called by God, it's going to come in some giant way, trumpets sounding, like the seas will part and there will be God with their mission.

It's not going to be that way. If that happens to you, please contact me and let me know because I'd want to hear that story! For most of us, it's a gentle whisper or nudge that the pieces of your life are finally falling into place at His time, for His glory.

RENA ELIZABETH SMITH: MY MOTHER

SMITH WAS my mother's maiden name. Rena Elizabeth was born in 1923, pre-depression. She was one of eight children. Her father, Henry, was a farmer in the Brimfield, Illinois area, not far from Peoria. His mother was from Germany, his father an American. Rena's mother, my grandmother, was Elizabeth. Her mother was also German, her father American. They were hard working, salt-of-the-earth people. Good German stock!

I don't remember them as well as I would like, but what

I do remember helps make my mother's story a little clearer to me the older I get. I remember going to their home many times when I was a boy and how much fun it was to hear my grandmother get mad about something and cuss people out in German. She spoke a lot of German in the house, but mainly in anger. I also remember that anytime she gave us something like a tin of cookies or a gift, if it was possible, she etched the exact date on the bottom. We always laughed about that as kids, but now I think she was smart in doing that. What better way to remember when you got it, providing you still have it? Of course, I have nothing from her today, just memories.

With my grandfather, I have some different memories. He was a very stern man, head full of silver hair and very tall, regal looking. They say he was about 6-foot-5. I remember once, he told me not to climb on a large retaining wall in their back-yard, which my cousins and I were climbing and jumping off. He had gone in the house and of course, I got back on the wall and the next thing I know, he grabs me by the hair and pulled me off the wall setting me down in the yard. I never got near that wall again.

Another key thing I remember about him was his visits to our house. I would be in the kitchen and always remembered my mom asking him, *"Is it a good day, Pop, or a bad day?"* I never really knew what they were talking about, but now believe she was asking more about his mood, not his health, as I never knew him to be sick. Looking back, I don't remember him as being a warm, loving grandfather figure, but one of sternness and seriousness; no playing around, ever. The weird part about all of that is, just before he died, he came to the house and opened his car trunk. There were fishing poles in the trunk and I said, *"It would be great to go fishing sometime with you."* He said, *"Yes, we should do that."* The next thing I knew, a week or so later he died suddenly and that was that.

• • •

Obviously, my mom had to have some sort of normalcy about her when my father met, fell in love with, and married her. She would have had to be someone worth loving, had to have some kind of attraction to him and they had to have some sort of common bond. I only knew her as the way she was, nothing normal at all. I only knew her as the sad, often crying and constantly sleeping woman who, on occasion, may have enjoyed something about the life she was living and the life she once knew in years past, long before marriage and her children. There were few times when she was jovial or in a great mood. It just wasn't there ninety percent of the time.

In my head, I keep looking for pieces of information or signs in past generations that mental illness was in our family and then handed down, as it most often is. I'll never really know if my grandfather or grandmother had any kind of diagnosed mental illness since all the siblings from mom's side of the family are all passed.

So, I like to think that my grandfather was the culprit on my mom's side. On my father's side, I knew of no one who I could distinctively say had the slightest mental illness. It makes more sense to me that it was on mom's side for sure. What I do remember is my mom telling me on many occasions that her parents were mean to her and punished her for many things, most of which she had no fault in the matter. She once told me that on one Christmas as the other children got presents, her parents gave her a box of potato peels because they said she didn't work as hard as her siblings. I can't even imagine such a thing, but I cannot remember my grandfather as a warm and caring person, only a stern and distant man.

• • •

As with many people who suffer with mental illness, their personal hygiene is lacking. They don't often bathe or shower, leave their hair unkempt, wear the same clothes every day without laundering, and don't brush their teeth. Sadly, my mother fit this description perfectly. So, you would wonder, why didn't my father push her more, encourage her more, or at least constantly seek help for her. I believe he did, as was evident before I was born as I was the direct result of the doctor's prescription of giving her another child to keep her busy and fulfilled. That was a true misdiagnosis if there ever was one for her, but for me it was a good thing, obviously.

Mom, like my son Chad, had a heart of gold. Her anger would well up in her, but she would take it out on only herself. Her constant wailing of *"I'm no good! I'm not good! I want to die!"* was proof of that. She really thought she was horrible and most often really did want to die. Her threats of suicide were constant. Even after I was married and moved out of the house, she would call Damara on the phone and wail those same words, *"I'm no good! I want to die!"* Damara worked third shift early in our marriage and it seemed mom liked to call her early in the morning, after I had gone to work, and Damara was just going to bed after working all night. In those days, you couldn't just unplug the phone. They were wired direct. You couldn't take the phone off the hook as then that loud alarm noise would come over the phone as warning the receiver was off the hook. There was no escape from it for poor Damara other than put a pillow over the receiver and her own head to quiet Rena's ranting. Damara would try to calm her down, but it didn't help. Mom would start out the conversation with her usual *"I want to die!"* She'd yell. *"I'm no good!"* and then reach a crescendo with loud crying and wailing into the receiver. It was maddening.

There was a time once, when I was around ten or twelve, when my mom was totally bedridden, and my dad thought she was actually going to die in that bed. She was totally incoherent to the world around her and was saying some very crazy things. One thing she said that I will always remember was, *"I see Jesus! He's calling to me! He wants me to come to him!"* Being the little smartass kid I was who had been through so many of these episodes with her, I asked her, *"Mom! Where do you see Jesus?"* She replied, *"He's there, standing at the corner at Workman's house!"* The Workman's lived on the corner and you could see their house and the corner clearly from our living room picture window. It was the most bizarre thing for her to say. I found myself looking and staring out that window looking for Jesus!

To help bring her out of this trance-like, zombie state she was in, my dad instructed my sister and I to get her out of bed and walk her back and forth across the downstairs. So, we did, from the living room to the kitchen and back. Walking her nonstop, back and forth, back and forth until she seemed to snap back to life. I don't know how many times we did this that day, but it seemed like all day. It was one of the weirdest things I can remember. I will never forget, though, that she saw Jesus standing at the corner by Workman's. Did she really she Him? I don't know. I can't say.

When my mother would be really nervous, she would sit on a chair or the sofa and grunt, methodically, pushing her hands back and forth on the top of her lap. She would at that same time, lean back and forth, like a rocking motion as she sat, grunting, and moaning, *"Ugh! Ugh! Ugh!"* like she was in a kind of internal pain. Physically she was not, but mentally she was in intense pain. I had seen other people do this in the psych ward when I would visit her during one of her stays, but it was scary to see her doing it all the time now. It was kind of like and Obsessive Compulsion Disorder (OCD). Over and over again she'd do this. She had many of those kinds of OCD things. She would literally count how many times she rinsed a washcloth or a piece of clothing in the sink. *"1, 2, 3, 4, 5, 6..."* Counting over and over again.

Mental illness is a disease of the mind, the brain, and it robs its victims of their sanity. This was so true in my mother's case. How I had wished and longed for just a normal mother/son conversation or being able to discuss anything with her of any reason. She was childlike in her manners, with her smile though, that made you sadly laugh inside because you just knew the ridiculousness of the whole situation, yet you still tried. You still tried, with the hope that someday, somehow, she would miraculously emerge from this hellish nightmare and be a normal person. It was never to be.

One thing, even in her tormented mind, she would give anything she had to try to help others. When charitable organizations called the house looking for volunteers, not knowing just whom they were talking with, my mother would answer the call and volunteer. Dad would have me go on those long walks around the neighborhood as she would walk up to a door, *Knock! Knock! Knock!* then the door would open and there we were! Rena and Roger! This tall, lanky, disheveled looking woman with wild, uncombed hair, mismatched hat and coat, holding hands with this little boy. *"Hello!"* mom would say, *"I'm collecting for Muspilcar Distroflees!"* Now, in reality, she was trying to say Muscular Dystrophy, but she could never get the words out right. I was amazed that she even tried. The person answering the door many times would laugh or look at her with pity. I could just sense and tell it. I swear I think they thought my mother was affected with the disease because she walked with fallen arches, her shoes scraped the ground and because of that, her knees knocking together as she walked. When she did the March of Dimes walks, they went a little better. Dad had me go along to try to help her with the money and to keep her from going out of our neighborhood. I felt like a little Forest Gump, handicapped not with leg braces, but handicapped in that I was responsible for my mother and not the other way around. C'mon mom, next house...

Rena Elizabeth Mohn

(December 23, 1923 – May 28, 2008)

The inner torment that was deep inside,
Was something you could never hide.

We loved you for who you were,
And you did your best, of that we're sure.

Your battles are over, your children are fine,
Now you're waiting for us and the passage of time.

We will meet again, of that we're certain,
When for us, too, God pulls the final curtain.

On that day, I will say to thee,
Yes, mom, I know that chicken died for me!

COOKING CLOTHES & OTHER GOODIES!

WE NEVER had a working clothes washing machine the whole time I was growing up. Dad would occasionally bring home a used wringer washer/tub machine, but more often than not, it would break and then it'd just sit in the backyard or get it hauled away. A clothes dryer? Forget it! That's what a clothesline was for, even in the dead of winter. I remember mom hanging clothes outside in the winter only to watch her bring them in, frozen stiff as a board, to hang them in front of a heat vent, to watch them collapse and lay on the floor. As a result of no washing machine, my mom basically cooked and boiled our clothes in a large pot on our kitchen stove. The pot was so encrusted with white lime that every once in a while, dad or my brother Ken, would need to scrape the inside of the pot to clean it. Hot water for anything had to be boiled on the stove as we rarely had hot water either, due to our water heater was mostly broken too. Are you seeing a pattern here? Mom would also heat pots and pots of hot water on the stove, so we could take baths and wash our hair. So, mom would cook the clothes, slopping water all over the kitchen floor, which eventually rotted out.

Many times, my dad would take my sister and me to the laundromat where we'd wash a week's worth of clothes on a Friday night. It was the one chance to get them done right and spare my mom from cooking them on the stove.

Dad wasn't into home maintenance, so his best fix for a rotting floor was to just cut a piece of plywood and nail it down over the hole. Our kitchen had a kaleidoscope of plywood patches all over it and to cover that up, they'd put small throw rugs everywhere. Our house was also so roach infested during my teenage years, when you turned on the kitchen light in the middle of the night it looked like the floor was moving, but in reality, it was the scurry of hundreds of roaches heading for cover. It was not a pleasant experience, but it was my reality. I always say today if I saw a roach in our home I'd rather burn down the entire house than try to exterminate them, because they are sheer hell to get rid of if deep infestation occurs. Fortunately, our children grew up in a very nice, great home, great neighborhood, which compared to what I grew up in, was outstanding luxury.

Now, two things here need to be said. My father, in addition to not making much money in his life (I out-earned him by age nineteen), the money he did have ended up in a beer bottle. So, do I hate my parents for all of this? For the love of God, NO! I loved them! I am totally confident that they did the very best they could, with what they had to work with and that was: THEMSELVES. They were both very uneducated and came from severe depression-era poverty. They had no real guidance in their lives either, growing up. Poverty usually begets poverty until someone somewhere breaks that cycle. When they were kids, they never had indoor plumbing, let alone an indoor bathroom. So, in their minds, they were doing alright. I totally understand their thought process and fully appreciate what they did teach us—honesty, for one, hard work, for another. My parents never stole anything, always told the truth, and worked hard for what they did have. My father, as much as a drinker that he was, always managed to get into work on time and work hard on his eight-hour shift. Alcohol aside, he was about as responsible as he could be considering everything I have known and experienced in my childhood.

• • •

In another example of how weird our home was growing up; my mother loved cats, many cats. In fact, at one time we had more than a couple dozen cats in our home. Yes, I know, you see that stuff on the TV show *Hoarders*. Our house was kind of like that, but not as bad as what you see on TV. The best I can say is our home was in a constant state of disarray. My brother and I, before school in the dead of winter, would have to shovel coal from the coal bin into the furnace to keep the house warm while we were in school. We were the last family in our neighborhood to still have a coal-stoked furnace.

Everyone else had converted to natural gas. I remember the stench of cat crap as I scooped a shovel-full of coal—and as it turns out, they used the coal bin like a litter box. We had cat crap all over the place. Inside the house, outside, everywhere, there was cat crap. We complained enough that eventually dad called the Animal Shelter and they came with boxes to load up those cats and haul them away. I remember sitting outside the house when the animal shelter workers came through with box after box of cats, their paws sticking out the side and lids, meowing and screaming.

One day I was in my office at the supermarket talking with one of my employees, Brian, telling him this cat story and he was like *"No way!"* So, as he was sitting there, I got my brother on the speakerphone. *"Ken!"* I said, *"Didn't we have 30 cats in the house when we were kids, and didn't the animal shelter come take them away?"* Ken smoothly replied, *"30 cats? No, it was only 22!"* Brian just about fell out of his chair with laughter, it was so funny. You just can't make these things up! They're too bizarre and off the wall.

Such is the life of any child growing up in a poor home with mental illness. Yes, it is sad because the child or children didn't choose their lot in life. We can't choose our parents; we can't choose where we are going to grow up. That's in God's hands. I didn't even think about God much the whole time I was growing up. We went to church up until the time I was about ten, then we stopped going. I asked my dad once, *"Why don't we go to church anymore?"* He said they changed the pastor and he didn't get along with the new guy. As an adult I have heard that same kind of thing from other people, whose parents quit taking them to church at about that age due to a change in the pastor and I have experienced that myself as an adult when a pastor was changed in the church we attended. It has only been in the last couple of decades that I have rediscovered God, His role in my life and how He has guided me. Especially these last few years, which has led me to write, confess my life, unbind my shame, share my story, and try to help others understand mental illness and how it affects families.

• • •

Mental illness is a tough disease. Sort of like an individual's cancer, or heart condition, it affects everyone in the house severely, as they will live with the affects that mental illness will have on that entire family. There is no escaping it other than leave the home entirely. You find yourself sometimes walking on eggshells as to not rile up or disturb the mentally ill person's emotions. It's a precarious way to live, far from a normal household.

The key is for those with mental illness to stay on those meds, continue to use therapy, and develop a support network of close friends and relatives to help keep them stable and guide them through any situations where they find themselves with high anxiety or other panic situations. If they know they can count on others to help them without judgment or prejudice, they will use that help when they need it.

• • •

These are the stories that I keep in me and I actually treasure them because without them, I have no other connection to my past. We weren't a close family and as my siblings and I grew into adults we drifted away from each other, yet we still live in the same area, just minutes from each other. I haven't seen my sister in several years and I may visit my brother every few months or so. I don't know why we don't keep the connection; I just know it's the way it is. Perhaps it's our way of severing the past, the way we grew up, the pain and shame inside us. We should have none of that, but I know I do, so they may as well. It's all perceived in our heads, or at least it is in mine. It's a tough thing to conquer sometimes. So many things like this can keep us all in some kind closet. Many times, I ask God for his guidance and deliverance to overcome these things and He always seems to get me through yet another hour, day, month, and year. You take it one step at a time, each and every day. Day-tight compartments.

TIMES PAST: IN REMEMBRANCE OF MY FATHER, THE VETERAN OF FOREIGN WARS

THEY SAY that things come and go in cycles. The cycle of payment for the freedoms we have so often taken for granted in our nation, comes due again and again in our terror-filled, chaotic world. I thank God for those that give of themselves, even their lives, to ensure us our freedom.

It wasn't so long ago that, at the end of the day on network television, they would sign off the air with things like displaying the flag gently waving against the blue sky, playing the Star-Spangled Banner with scenes of Air Force jets flying across the sky with their exhaust trails streaming across our TV screen.

Years ago, as a child, I used to watch my father on so many occasions rise out of his chair and fully salute the television screen at those times. He would make me do it do, too, and I will admit now that, at the time, I used to almost think it funny. I would never laugh at him about it, though, because somehow the intensity of his devotion in that silly nightly ritual told me that if I had made fun of it, he would have clobbered me.

My father was a World War II veteran. He was born in 1917 and served in the U.S. Army from the beginning of World War II in 1941 until its end in 1945. He served in what was called the European Theatre, which included almost the entire European Continent. Post-war, my father was also a member of the VFW (Veterans of Foreign Wars), Post 8662. As I previously explained, I spent many a day and night in that building. I always tell people and especially my children that I grew up in the VFW. My memories of the VFW Hall on Garden Street in the south end of Peoria are just as vivid to me today as they were back then.

The men, all veterans, became my friends and included a colorful cast of characters, such as guys named Sweet Pea, Curly, and Cotton, to name a few. I knew most of them by their last names only, such as Berkey, Miller, or Jones. They even had a bowling league that bowled on Mondays. I especially enjoyed Mondays because Dad would take me bowling with him and all the guys would give me Pepsi's and candy while I watched them bowl and did my homework. I felt like their club mascot so many times in that smoke-filled bowling alley.

As a stupid, snot-nosed kid, I wasn't mature enough to appreciate my father's war experiences nor did I view his involvement in the VFW as anything important. To me then, the VFW was more a social club than an important organization dedicated to the memory and well-being of all our war veterans.

It wasn't until much later in my life that I realized how important this organization was, not only to my father, but all veterans. I remember the parades, the color guards, and the pride on the faces of each of them as they talked about serving their country.

My father passed away on June 14, 1994, at age 77. He only had an eighth-grade education but was smarter than many college graduates. He never achieved greatness in any material sense of the word, but he did achieve greatness in my eyes and especially on September 11, 2001, when we all watched in horror what was unfolding in our nation on that crisp, cool, and sunny Tuesday morning. That day has made me realize and be so very thankful that somewhere in the world, during World War II, he helped make a difference and served his country, as so many of our patriots have, ensuring our freedom; those same freedoms that are now under attack today here and across the world.

No, he wasn't a highly decorated war hero who saved an entire platoon. No, he didn't carry his best friend through enemy fire. He did honor his country by answering its call to duty with pride and honor. He served his nation as thousands of others did during some of the toughest times in our history.

He did instill in his children that pride for his country. In his role at the VFW, he was twice a post commander and then a chaplain, which was for me hard to understand because of his alcoholism and heavy lifestyle. The reality of his position as chaplain hit me the day I got to sit through a meeting and my father opened the meeting with a prayer. It was the first time I had heard my father lead a group in prayer in public. I was literally stunned as I listened to him so eloquently, so together, in saying that prayer. It seriously brought tears to my eyes and I never, ever told him about it. I was totally amazed. Today, my son, Chad, with all the bipolar and personality issues he has in his life, can pray like my father; the right words filling his spirit and saying just the right things at the right times. It is truly a gift from God.

The Circle

Life has a strange way of separating the lives,
Of people who were once close in each other's eyes.

Children grow up so fast and become parents of their own,
As grandparents instill in them, the values that they've known.

Life is so short anyway that there is seldom time to stop,
And reflect back on the good times, that togetherness once brought.

Life is indeed a circle from the beginning until the end,
And that rule will never break, although sometimes it will bend.

As our life's circle will just as certainly come to a close,
We seldom get to know just when, for it is God who really knows.

Remember to tell others that we love them, even though we are apart,
Because you may never get a second chance to mend a broken heart.

Roger L. Mohn
1994

WAS IT DEPRESSION?

Early in my life, I knew depression. I didn't really have a name for it nor realized how much I was depressed; I only knew I was sad, lonely, withdrawn, and prone to sleep a lot, much like my mother during my teenage years. I was a skinny little white kid bullied at school, my lunch money taken almost daily by black thugs who cornered me, even in the classroom, and my teachers did nothing to stop it. Shop class was the worst, as the teacher was always in another area when it happened. I was attacked once while walking from my locker to homeroom. I was decked to the floor by a sucker punch out of nowhere as I was walking with my friends. It happened so fast and so hard, I didn't really know who hit me, only that I found myself, face to floor, watching my homeroom band class drumsticks roll across the floor as my attackers lined the hall on both sides yelling in pleasure that they decked me. With my face still on the floor, as I watched those drumsticks roll away, I also saw my friends abandon me and run as fast as they could down the hall to escape themselves. It was the early 1970s and the nation was still struggling with race and equal rights. It seemed like one of the rights those black kids did have was bullying me to no end. I picked myself up, gathered my books and drumsticks, listening to the laughter around me, and instead of going to class, I walked out the door and went home. I'd had enough. No one was going to stop it. I didn't have the courage to do it myself and I look back at that time with shame for not standing up for myself and taking the abuse that I did. It was *turning the other cheek* to an extreme, if nothing else.

It was pretty much the beginning of the end of my school career and would lead to the biggest regret of my life—that I gave in to fear and failure, accepting less of myself than I knew I was capable of. My grades were always great when I was in school and the counselors did their best to encourage me, but I'd had enough.

I came from the poor side of town and without the motivation or seeing anyone around me achieve success; I had no role model or examples of what I could become with hard work and the proper motivation in my life. In my heart, I felt hopeless, sank into despair, and just started skipping school altogether. Looking back, I put as much effort into skipping school as I probably would have done just staying there for the long haul, but it wasn't in the cards for me. Not now.

I would get up for school, get ready, and go there, only to end up walking back out that door to head home. It was weird, yes, but it's just the way it was. At home, if my mother wasn't in the hospital for one of her many breakdowns, I could stay at home in an empty house, upstairs. But if she was at home, I would hide out in the basement, so she wouldn't know I was there. I drank nothing or ate nothing the whole day, so no need to use the bathroom. We had no bathroom in the basement. I can't even explain it to this day other than perhaps to say it was my way of escaping the world around me.

It was my way of hiding from the world, as I did little to help myself at the time to overcome the obstacles in front of me. I just wasn't capable at the time, mentally, and certainly not maturely. I don't know what really changed later, only the fact that I needed to make money, so I decided instead of staying in school, I would drop out and work full time. I was working at Kroger at the time and I know they needed good full-time help. I spoke to my manager and he said he would take me on full time if I did quit school, so I made the decision. A big mistake, but it's what I did perhaps to escape into a different life than the one I was living. Looking back, it all seems so bizarre to me, because the person I was then and the person I became are so far apart. I grew up, matured, and evolved based on forgiveness with the past. It was that past that I now understand was meant to be, to bring me to where I am now.

I know if I had one of my employees come to me with that same request, asking if they dropped out of school would I offer them full-time employment, I would have not held that carrot out for them, but do everything in my power to talk them back into school. I would never offer them a full-time job as an enticement to quit school. It'd be insane to even think about now. That's why it was so important and never an option for our children to drop out of school and two of our children have full, four-year college degrees, of which I am very proud. It was a long way from my stupid decision to drop out of high school, later getting my G.E.D, and a very long way from my parent's eighth-grade educations. In the meantime, as I worked my way into management and eventually owning our own company, I had taken numerous self-help courses like Dale Carnegie, Zig Ziglar, Tony Robbins, and also read so many books and seminars by these self-help gurus as well.

In my turbulent youth, I had not yet known or found God, had not yet developed faith in Him, or myself obviously, nor did I have much hope for a future beyond my current situation. I was about as far away from God as anyone could be. He was not even on my mind.

IT'S IN THE GENES, AND THEN SOME

BY THE time I was nineteen years old, I had been married and divorced. I was pretty much the example of what not to do in your teenage years. I was seventeen years old, she was fifteen and she became pregnant. Horrible, yes, I know, but I wanted to do the right thing, which I thought was getting married, at the time, so we married. I think we thought we were in love, but it was an immature love, with no depth or much thought about how the future would turn out. The marriage lasted about eighteen months before ending badly. I would eventually discover that both her parents had mental health issues. In my family, it was mom. In hers, it was both mother and father. My son, Chad, with his bipolar issues, didn't stand a chance in that mix of genes from both sides of the family. In any given family, if one parent has a mental illness, there is about a twenty-five percent chance that it will be passed on to a child. If both parents have issues, then that statistic goes up to about to fifty to seventy-five percent. Both of Chad's grandmothers were bipolar, his grandfather was bipolar and his mother as well. It was recipe for mental illness.

Soon into the marriage, I realized I had made huge mistake and there was no way it could go on. Chad's mother also had severe issues of her own. As things began to fall apart, I decided to divorce and push for full custody of my son and do everything I could to make that happen. I convinced his mother and a judge that I would be the best parent and in 1976, I was granted full custody, allowing her visitation rights every other weekend. His mother never even went to court once. This was in a time when a father was rarely granted full custody rights, let alone a poor, uneducated teenage father, who was now a high school dropout, but with a good fulltime job. Looking back, I still can't believe I convinced that judge, let alone her, to agree.

Chad's childhood during our brief marriage was very turbulent. He witnessed his mother and I arguing constantly. Full-blown yelling and screaming for the roughly eighteen months we were together. It was immature for both of us, but then again, we were uneducated teenagers lacking in role models on either side of the family.

I began working full time when I was seventeen, so the biggest issue I had after our divorce was caring for Chad while I was at work. Although I was making decent money, out-earning my father by age nineteen, I still did not have much money for a full-time sitter. I had to opt for my mother. I thought I could control the situation, plus my mother had been very stable for a little while at that time so I made the decision to trust her to babysit Chad. I think the responsibility of helping to care for Chad helped keep her more stable, but I knew I was gambling with my son's well-being. Not that she would ever hurt Chad, but her sadness and depression would become a factor in my decision to eventually seek another option for his care while I worked. I was making more money as I had just been promoted into a supervisor's position.

In the divorce, Chad's mother was granted visits every other weekend, but she rarely exercised those rights, and, in the end, it was best. She would call me up and say she was going to take him for the weekend and I would have Chad ready to go, but then she wouldn't show up. Sometimes she'd call to say she couldn't make it after all, but many times she just wouldn't show up and little Chad would be there with all his things ready to go see his mom, his coat on, all set and then I'd have to tell him some story as to why she couldn't make it. It happened many, many times. She had no job, no means of support and no car. Of course, she was also very young, like me, but had no drive to improve herself or her situation.

The best thing that eventually happened is she married a guy in the military and they moved to far away to places like Hawaii and Texas, so the disappointment of her not showing up was over and the worry of that situation was gone. It was just me and Chad and it was fine.

I'm not proud of how it was back then, but I am proud of how we came through it. But, Chad is still bipolar, and he will be for life. This is fact. You just don't erase mental illness. It's always there, but you can surely manage it with the proper meds, counseling, and support group help when needed. There are so many people out there with mental illnesses that come from great homes, great backgrounds, and still manage to have mental illness surface in their lives. Mental illness is an equal opportunity illness. You can be rich, poor, uneducated, or even have a Ph.D. If you do have mental illness anywhere in your ancestry, there's a chance someone in your immediate family or a generation into the future may find themselves with it. When my wife and I talked with Patty Duke that was one thing she said to us, that she watched her grandchildren very closely for signs of trouble. Keep in mind my past reference to the Hemmingway's family legacy.

• • •

Fast-forward another couple of years and I met someone who would change my life and Chad's forever, for the better. In the summer of '79, Damara Wagner came into our lives. She had just graduated high school, just eighteen years old. It's just so hard to imagine it all back then when I think about our children at that age and how totally not-ready-for-prime-time-life we were. Nonetheless, I was smitten with her and we were married the following year. We've been married thirty-eight years and counting as I write this, with three more children of our own. Damara was a tough disciplinarian with Chad right out of the gate and she had to be. In my mind, I gave Chad too much slack because I always felt bad and guilty of how things were for him. He didn't need that. He needed tough love and with Damara, he got exactly that. It helped, but Chad's problems were surfacing and over the next several years they would escalate into full-blown bipolar disorder. Chad was just five years old when I met Damara.

I was too naïve to really see it back then and I think I didn't want to, either. I never imagined him being bipolar, only having behavior problems. I was wrong, completely wrong.

Chad grew into a man, but overall, effectively remains stuck in his emotions and many of his thought processes are closer to a teenager or adolescent. NAMI taught me that many times, whatever age a person is when the illness surfaces, they can stay stuck at that age and maturity level. This is most certainly true with Chad. Now forty-four years old, he is very intelligent and can spout major sport facts and statistics that I could only dream about, but his emotional maturity level is stuck somewhat as an adolescent/teenager. Unable to hold a job for any length of time, he is listed as mentally disabled, on SSDI (Social Security Disability Income), and has a payee through the local Human Service Center who takes care of his housing, food, and necessities. Every time he does land a job, within days or weeks he loses it because he cannot control his emotions, gets upset if anyone even looks at him wrong or tries to give him constructive advice and he usually walks out of the place. He has worked just about every kind of part-time job a person can work. He interviews well, gets hired, and then things fall apart. It's the illness, but also his lack of discipline to stay on the meds and seek fast help when he needs it. Then it just spirals out of control. He is a good, fast worker, however, if kept to task. I thank God that He has protected Chad from not only himself but others who would take advantage of his generous and caring heart.

This is pretty much the same type of story that many people with mental illness affecting a loved one can testify too. It's a vicious cycle that repeats itself over and over and over again. Things go great for a time and then fall apart. More often than not it comes down to staying on the meds. Once they feel great, as I have said, they feel so confident they abandon the meds and then the nasty cycle starts all over again.

Chad has a heart of gold but can also be a master of manipulation, a common trait of mental illness. Lying and sadly, stealing from loved ones can and does happen. In our experience, we've had more of the lying to us, never the stealing. Chad can look you straight in the eyes with confidence and lie right to you and do his best to convince you he's absolutely telling the truth. It is the illness. Fortunately for us, because he does have that heart of gold, the depth into his eyes reveal he is lying. We just know. To set the record straight, it may look like I am attacking Chad in this book, but I have talked to him about my writing a book about our relationship, his illness, and he is at peace with it. He even offered to speak with me about it in public and that would be a very bold move, one that I hope he follows through with.

I am very proud of him, in all of this. I know it's not at all easy for him and I love him so much for the battle he fights in his head every day. It takes a strong person to keep that up.

When Chad was a child, he would have severe behavior issues and I never even suspected any kind of a mental illness, only disciplinary problems. Because of this, his siblings were affected by his behaviors. We did our very best to try to control the situation as much as we could, but inevitably, the whole family is affected.

As Chad grew older, the problems escalated. There was a disruption at every family event we attended and usually we ended up leaving early to handle Chad's behavior or we drove separately so I could leave with Chad if necessary. That's just the way it was and became. There were times, of course, when things came together, we had a great time, and all was well, but those times were far and few between unfortunately.

I give Damara the credit of being a disciplinary saint during these times as she had motherhood thrown at her so young and did the very best she could. I am amazed we made it through it all.

CHAD'S STRUGGLE FOR SANITY

BY THE time Chad was in his early teens, the behavior problems escalated. We could see it earlier than that, so we went to counseling at those times to help work the problem, even having him in special classes when available, but the issues would resurface time and time again. When he was a small boy, he would have temper tantrums, hit himself, pull out his hair and/or kick and scream. No matter how we reacted, it was always this cycle of misbehavior, over and over again.

Once in junior high school he had an altercation with a

classmate and ended up hitting the kid, causing the kid to fall and break his arm. We were glad that was all the physical damage that was done, but it was enough to get Chad kicked out of school for a bit. It was also one of the very few times that Chad's violence was directed at someone other than himself. He made threats of violence against us, but he also knew his limitations and we were fully prepared to do whatever necessary to protect our family against any harm he may try to inflict.

One time, though, when he was in his early teens, Chad borrowed some butcher knives from an old man in our neighborhood, telling the man, *"My dad needs some knives for the store. Can he borrow some from you?"* Since we owned the local grocery store, the old gentleman was a good customer and knew my wife and me. Later, he told us he thought it was odd that I would need to send Chad out around the neighborhood to borrow knives to use at our store, but since he knew us, and thought we needed the knives, he never questioned Chad's intent. What happened after Chad borrowed the knives is something we'll never forget.

We had an argument with Chad, one of so many, that day and ultimately, he took off from home, mad, and left to run the neighborhood. Damara was at a local lady's event and I was home with Chad's siblings, Christopher, Roger Jr., and Elizabeth. They were very young at the time, maybe 5, 4, and 1 years old, respectively. After dark, with the butcher knives in hand, Chad came back to the house, and standing on the outdoor cellar door just outside the kitchen window, jumped up and down with the knives in his hands screaming at the top of his lungs, *"I am going to kill you all! I am going to kill you all!"* His brothers were the first to see him and screamed. I ran into the kitchen, saw him, and then without thinking ran out the door after him. He ran away fast into the dark night. I could not catch him or see which way he went.

I immediately called the police and they began their hunt for him. He was found, and then brought back home. Since he was a juvenile, the police thought it was best that he be returned back home to us to work it all out.

The next day started with arguments about his behavior. Then Chad got mad again, darted out of the house, and began cruising the neighborhood on his bike. I then, like a crazed idiot, got in my car and tried to chase him down to bring him home. After about an hour of him evading me on that bicycle, I decided I would grab a bike and go after him, but once I got home I could not pick up his trail again as there were plenty of places to go hide, even in a small town. I did ride my bike for a while, hoping I would find him. I look back at all of this and it was pretty dumb on my part, but I had just had enough of his bad behavior and my emotions got the best of me, unfortunately. The whole thing was a nightmare.

A few hours later, he did come home, still pissed off, and arguing. He made some threats and I grabbed him and as he pushed me away, my arm hit his nose and he got a nose bleed. He took off again from our back porch and I jumped off the porch after him. It was then that I felt a pain so sharp and something snap in the back of my calf. I went down for the count right there in the backyard, while Chad ran blocks away as fast as he could.

He then flagged down our local police officer and told him that I punched him in the face, which was a lie, as Damara was standing right there when it happened and was witness to what happened. I would never touch any of my children that way. Swat their ass with my bare hand or a belt, yes, but never punch them in the face.

The officer then took Chad to the town hall, which also doubled as the police station. The officer called my wife and I and we went to meet him and Chad there. We did our best to refute Chad's story, but the officer was bound by law to call the Department of Child Care and Family Service (DCFS) to have them present in any case of alleged child abuse. It was pure rubbish, but nonetheless they were called. They had to come from twenty-five miles away and the wait took forever. In that time all we could do was stay quiet and sit it out.

Once they arrived, the interrogation of us began. They asked Chad all sorts of things in private and then in front of us. It was utterly humiliating, but we know the law and just did the best we could to convey that Chad had severe behavior issues. They then began talking about taking our other three children away from us, pending a full investigation; for fear that we may be abusive parents. That crossed the line for Damara, who is not Chad's biological mother but basically the only mother he had. She began to cry, plead, then get really pissed that Chad's own behavior brought us all to this mess. Damara told them, *"I'll be damned if Chad's behavior, threatening us and his siblings with knives, saying he's going to kill us all, gets our children taken away! Over my dead body that will ever happen!"* It was the last straw for her and me too. It just became too much. We'd been through all kinds of child counseling, behavior goal setting, time-outs, that parents could do. I think it was at this point that the DCFS rep could see that Chad's behavior was the real culprit in the issue and they began to believe us.

No matter though, it was their job to separate Chad from us temporarily for a cooling-off period of three to seven days. They took him to a foster home in the Quad Cities, some twenty-five miles away. It gave him and us a chance to cool down, regroup and reflect about what was to come next. During that time, Chad's temporary foster home talked with him about his behavior and made him do chores in their home, which he wasn't too excited about, he would later tell us.

Unfortunately, in my pursuit of trying to find Chad that day and riding that bicycle in that pursuit, when I jumped off the porch to try to catch Chad, I felt a sharp snapping pain in my left calf. It took me down to my knees in pain. I thought I had sprained my leg. It took ten more days in agonizing pain to learn what I had really done.

That night after our interview at the police station and DCFS's decision to remove Chad for a few days from us, we went home, and I had unbearable pain in my calf. By this time, the back of my calf was black and blue, swollen up badly. I could barely walk. Damara wrapped my leg in an Ace bandage and that helped a bit, at least I could walk a little.

The next day I went to visit our local doctor, who happened to have his clinic on the next block from our home. It was a short, but painful walk.

He was a family practitioner and he also thought I had sprained my leg or pulled a muscle. He gave me pain pills, wrapped me back up, and sent me on my way. Over the next ten days it just got worse. The pain was so intense and the only way I could walk was with my calf totally wrapped tight and then I could only stand up for minutes at a time.

On the tenth day, I went back to the doctor. The bruising looked worse and he decided to send me to the Quad Cities to the sports doctor who worked with the Quad City Thunder basketball team. I went there the very next day.

As I sat on the gurney the doctor took off the wrappings and looked at my swollen, darkly bruised calf. He asked me, *"Now how long has it been like this?"* I told him it happened ten days prior. He couldn't believe it. He said to me, *"Do you know what you've done?"* *"No, what?"* I asked.

"You've severed your Achilles tendon! The bruising and pain you have is because it's like a rubber band and it has snapped back up into your calf!" Then he said, *"Feel the back of your ankle on your good leg. Then feel the back of your ankle on the injured leg. See, your tendon is gone on the injured leg."* It was the weirdest feeling realizing that I had no tendon attached to the back of my ankle. *"What does this mean?"* I asked.

"That means surgery tomorrow morning, ASAP!" The rest is pretty much history. They reattached my tendon. I spent the first week or so confined to our sofa, leg elevated 24/7. They had me on crutches for another three weeks. During that time, I went to work, cut meat on crutches, and ran my stores. It was not fun. After about a month, they put a walking stump on the cast and I was able to walk a little better. Six weeks out, the cast was removed, and I then spent another six weeks in strength therapy to build the leg back up. In all this, I had no one to blame but myself. Had I just stayed calm, not reacted as I did, and not jumped off that porch; I would have saved my tendon and a ton of time and money.

Upon Chad's return home, his siblings were very apprehensive being around him. Even though he apologized to us all, the damage was done. It's hard to erase the memory of your brother staring at you through a window, in the dark of night, brandishing knives and yelling he was going to kill us all. No, it just doesn't go away that easily.

• • •

One of many issues people with mental illnesses have to deal with after they go through their manic or psychotic episodes and usually don't understand or come to terms with, is the horrible things they may say or do to those they love. They just can't take it back. It's like the genie is out of the bottle and you can't put it back in. They can apologize a hundred times and you can forgive them seventy x seven, but it's still there. Chances are it will happen again and again. It's just part of their mental illness and part of the ongoing struggle that they must work to control. We, as their family and friends, must learn our own ways of understanding their illness and coping with it. That's the great thing about NAMI. They offer free Basic and Family-to-Family classes, taught by people just like us, on how to work through these kinds of situations. I didn't even know NAMI existed until Chad had long moved out of our home. For me, it was an eye opener in knowing I was not alone in any of this; others have walked the same road Damara and I had.

As Chad grew older, the bouts with his temper and acting up got better. Besides the impact it had on his own sanity; the impact on his brothers and sister was also not good at all. They have long forgiven him for anything he'd done over the years and have fully accepted him and his illness.

Today, Chad is doing well in keeping his illness under control. He's staying on his meds and working a part-time, seasonal job, which works out great for him, as holding down a regular job is almost next to impossible for him. He is in a relationship with someone who also has issues of her own, but they make the relationship work to the best for both of them and we are happy about that. He has come a very long way from where he was before.

NAMI
The Saving Grace

My involvement in NAMI (National Alliance on Mental Illness) changed my life, opened my eyes, and helped educate me about the struggles of mental illness, a journey I am still on and will be on forever. Mental illness doesn't just go away—if you have it, you have it for life. But in most cases it can be managed with medications and therapy, which is the good news.

I spent much of my life hiding in my self-imposed closet, full of shame about our family's secret of mental illness, as if I had been personally responsible for it. That's the effect it can have on you. You work hard at living a double life, the one the public sees and knows versus the real one that you deal with every day. It's always there.

It's time to break the bonds of this malady and educate everyone that mental illness is a true disease and there should be no shame in it. There has been such a negative attitude by the public and the media toward anyone with mental illness because it has been such a mystery, not only in its diagnosis, but in the proper treatment of it.

If I Could Do It Over

If I could do Fatherhood over, here are some things I'd do,
From the moment of your birth, I'd always be there for you.
From the time you took your first step, until you caught your first
    ball,
I would promise to be the best father, the finest of them all.

I would never say that I am too busy, or turn my head away,
If you wanted me to talk to you, or if you just wanted to play.
I realize now, too late in life, that we seldom "baited a hook,"
Or how little time we spent, curled up together, reading you a book.

There were times when I was guilty, of looking ahead in time,
To when you would be grown and gone, and I know now that was a
    crime.
Now I realize how much I missed as I spent so much time at the
    store,
As I am now filled with regret, that of my time, you didn't get much,
    much more.

I never knew how much I would miss just watching you sleep at
    night,
Or how much I would long to hear, you and your siblings fight.
If I could do it over, I would try my very best to control my temper
    when mad,
Because I wouldn't want you to be "just like me" when you became
    a dad.

I wish I had paid attention to TV Dads like Danny Thomas and my
    hero, Ward Cleaver,
And studied the meanings and messages in family shows like
    "Leave it to Beaver."

It's times like these that I realize the mistakes that I often made,
And the fears that I have failed you are the things that make me
    afraid.

I am afraid that through my actions, I have taught you to be like me,
And that is what bothers me most, because it is now that I really
    see.
I see that through the years I have been so wrong about so many,
    many things,
I only pray that you did learn right from wrong, no matter what the
    future brings.

If I could only do it over, I would realize how fast time goes by,
And that the time we have together would be gone in the blink of
    an eye.
I would treat each day, each hour, each minute that I did spent with
    you,
As a time we would only have once, knowing how soon it would be
    through.

I would prepare myself, before you were even born, to do the best I
    could do,
Because I know now that everything inside of me, will someday be
    in you.

MY OWN BATTLE

NOW I will get into my own personal struggles with depression. I have experienced it several times in my life over the years, from adolescence through adulthood. I can only say when it hits you, it's like nothing else matters. You suddenly lose all hope, your energy and the drive, sometimes, to even stay alive. I know it sounds deep and weird, but it's true. You just want the sadness to end and somehow it doesn't. As I have said earlier, mental illness is an equal opportunity disease. It affects the poor and rich, the highly educated and the uneducated alike. It affects the super talented and untalented. Just because someone seemingly has everything in life anyone else could ever want, doesn't mean that person is happy and is not struggling with their own kind of personal hell at times. Look at all the Hollywood celebrities, musicians, actors, and comedians that have confessed to some type of mental illness and or committed suicide because in the end, they just couldn't overcome it.

I can relate to it. On the surface, it can appear that I have the world by the tail, but in my head, I can hear my mother's voice as she told herself she was no good, no good to anyone, that she wanted to die so many times. I hear that in my head from time to time, those same feelings, those same thoughts and it's hard to fight it. I think as a kid I was subliminally conditioned for it by my mother's constant battle with her own sanity. Realistically, I know it will pass, but mentally, it's still there. It's just not something that you can easily block out and just pull yourself together from when it hits you. Those that can't understand it will say things like *"Get out of your own damn pity party!"* or *"Quit feeling sorry for yourself!"* Neither is applicable.

It comes on like a speeding train but lingers like the slow drip of water on your head like Chinese water torture; only it's in your head. I've also conditioned myself, in these times, to do the very best I can in putting on my happy face, getting out there and doing whatever it takes to give all the appearances that I am fine, when inside I may be in severe depression mode. It puts a whole new meaning to the phrase, "To thine own self be true!" because in essence, you're lying to yourself, but you know the sadness will pass and you'll do anything to keep moving forward until it does. It's hard to explain unless you, too, have been through it. It's why so many comedians have some type of depression or bipolar in their background. My sense of humor has been my constant companion throughout my life and has brought me back from the brink of depression and thoughts of suicide many times. It's exactly why I need to "come out" now, out of this self-imposed closet of shame, confess, and share my story as I know there are so many others who are dealing with this exact same thing. I've heard their stories and shared their pain.

. . .

Just a few years ago, my wife and I lost our business after twenty-two years of owning and operating it, raising our family with it. It was our life and livelihood. Unless you have owned a business and lost it, you'd never understand the impact that has on you. My wife and I both worked it and drew our income from it. When we had to close it, not only I lost my job, she did too. Today, we have learned to live on about forty percent of what we once earned together and yet, we are blessed. Fortunately, our children were grown and our last child, our daughter was just moving out of the house. In retrospect, it was time. The business had been failing the last several years and it was bound to crash. Many people go through the loss of a business. They say that when you lose a business after a long time of owning it, it's like the death of a close family member. For us, it was and for me, it was traumatic. You second guess yourself every day with things you tried to do, things you could have done to hopefully prevent its demise. In the end, nothing worked, and we knew it was inevitable.

I had been my own boss, my own motivator and motivating those that worked for us for twenty-two years. Then I found myself, after two decades, working for someone else, taking orders from someone else and believe me, after you call your own shots for decades in a business of your own, going to work for someone else is a very rough and humbling experience. You end up drinking up someone else's proverbial Kool-Aid after you've been serving your own to others for decades. Sometimes you don't want to drink that Kool-Aid because of your own engrained thoughts and talents, but you do. You must. Then you realize their Kool-Aid isn't bad, just different. OK, enough metaphors. No one in your new company cares about all the business experience, management experience and leadership ability you have. You weren't hired for that ability, so it means nothing and that is tough to come to terms with. I've bought millions of dollars' worth of equipment, inventory and supplies, hired hundreds of people, worked with a multi-million-dollar annual budget, did much of my own daily accounting and general ledger work. It means nothing anymore. They only know that you had a small business that failed, so somehow you must not have been good enough to keep it going. That is the negative stuff you fill your head with whether it's true or not what others think. You shouldn't care about that junk, but the reality is you can't help it sometimes. In the process, I developed my own brand of depression and PTSD (Post Traumatic Stress Disorder). I ended up in counseling to help deal with it all.

As I look back, I firmly believe God closed that door, as painful as it was, to open a new opportunity, to push me into something I should have been doing all along. To write, to speak in public and become an advocate for those with mental illness. It now makes perfect sense, but at that time of our closing, it was the furthest thing in my mind. So, God puts me in the book manufacturing business. In this, I learn so much and regain the lost confidence in myself that I once had in the prime of my business days. I meet people who can help others in their pursuit of getting their own books and stories published. I partner those people together and I've got to see some great books published and the excitement and satisfaction in that has been awesome. Thank you, Lord! So here I am, now with my own book, sharing some things that so many others deal with, each in their own way, each story is unique to them and their family.

Those of you who have never been through this or have been fortunate enough not to have it in your family, cannot even fathom to understand it. To you, it would look like anyone with this in their head is weak and has severe character flaws, but nothing could be further from the truth. I think those of us who suffer with this thing yet keep it at bay and in control ninety-eight percent of the time, are actually stronger than the rest. And that probably doesn't make sense either, but I know in my heart it's true. I have heard so many people talk about those with mental illnesses as if there are something less than human, something that should be shunned, and the person locked away. I've been in the company of fools who, to define their own self-worth and importance, have made fun and ridiculed those with mental illness. I know this because in my distant past, even though my mother suffered greatly, at times I was one of those ignorant people. It was part of my coping with it, I think. I think it's some kind of a sick defense mechanism to justify our own worth, our own confidence that we *aren't like those people*, when the reality is that one out of four or five people will suffer some type of a mental illness in their lifetime. That's kind of scary to think about, but it is true.

They say these things because they can't come to grips with the fact that mental illnesses are a real disease, as debilitating as any other kind of physical disease, only with mental illness, it's so hard to get an accurate diagnosis. There's no 100 percent accurate blood test, no accurate brain scan, no test that can pinpoint what exactly is going on. Diagnosis is done by observation and discussion with the person, their family, and friends.

• • •

Once after giving a talk and sharing some of these things in public via NAMI, I was in Chicago at a convention when I learned that someone from Peoria needed a ride home and I was leaving to head home myself. This person had heard me talk about thoughts of suicide and asked me point blank, "How do you feel tonight?" as he was concerned I may run the car off the road and kill us both. It was so intensely funny but at the same time, so insanely real because this person also deals with his own mental illness and for him, he just wanted to be sure I was OK, or least for the ride home. We laughed about it after he said it and it became a good conversation piece for some time after that night, as I ended up sharing the conversation we had with others in my talks. It was so surreal, yet so to-the-point.

The kicker is, I try to keep my faith intact, my trust in God that all will be well, but even with all that, during the darkest of hours, in those turbulent times, it seems like my faith, along with my positive, enthusiastic personality, can go temporarily out the window. My faith in God has also brought me through those dark times and I can honestly say that God had His hand on me the entire time, and He will use this, as he does so often, for His glory and purpose. In that I am confident and secure. It is why at this point in my life, I have decided to share my story, my thoughts in the hope that someone else can benefit and gain some insight into the struggles of mental illness. That someone reading this book can either relate to it themselves or knows someone else who needs to know they are not alone in their struggle for sanity.

In sharing my story, I know I risk ridicule by those who cannot understand mental illness, but it doesn't matter anymore, I have to get out of this different kind of closet and talk about it more in public. Since this book has taken years to come together, recently in the news two very popular celebrities, Kate Spade and Anthony Bourdain took their own lives within days of each other, and it pretty much shocked and rocked the public. This doesn't shock and rock me, however; because those thoughts have run through my own head and I work hard to keep those negative thoughts at bay. From the outside looking in, those two people had so much to live for—success, fame, wealth, and purpose. In their minds, though, I am sure they struggled with so much doubt, fear, and self-destructing thoughts that in the end they felt the only way to end the inner "brain-pain" was to end their lives. It's a sad commentary because I am sure they felt that coming forward and going very public with their struggles would be looked upon as weak or as attention-getting, possibly wrecking their image, but the down side is that suffering in silence, not seeking the proper help can only cause the problem to spiral out of control.

Each time, when those negative thoughts are there, I pray to God, *"Please, Lord, save me from myself! Save me from the self-defeating negative thoughts that so easily creep into my head. Save me from self-destruction and use my life as a testimony to others that they may overcome those same thoughts."* Just as I put in the front of this book, my favorite verse from the Bible, *"For I know the plans I have for you,"* declares the Lord, *"plans to prosper you and not harm you, plans to give you hope and a future."* –Jeremiah 29:11. That verse has gotten me through so many rough times.

I think I had heard my mother, in her tears and crying pain, tell me that she was worthless, no good, and wanted to die, with a butcher knife at her throat so many, many times, that somehow those same thoughts roll through my head because I am her son. It's about the only way I can justify and explain it after all these years. In part, I feel like I have wasted a huge part of my life because I could have been out there helping, motivating, and speaking in public to others who suffer with these same thoughts so much sooner. It is a goal of mine at this stage of my life, to come out of this self-imposed closet of make-believe shame and help others suffering in the same silence I spent decades in and still do. I can't say this enough: There is no longer a need to suffer in silence.

• • •

If you are struggling, feeling lost, hopeless and in despair, remember this: YOU ARE NOT ALONE! One out of every four or five of us, seriously, deal with a mental health issue, although many will never admit it for the negative impact it usually has. So, in the United States with a population of well over 300 million has, at any given time, at least 75 million people with mental health issues of some sort. Even more staggering is the fact that we push mental health treatment and funding to the back burner of needed healthcare, like it's something that doesn't really need the same importance as other medical illnesses like heart disease, cancer, or whatever. It's sad, as we wonder why so many people who end up using horrific violence against others or themselves, got to that state of mind. Why? How?

Before you do something that is a *permanent decision to a temporary situation*, like suicide, please reach out to someone, anyone, to let them know you're struggling. Call the numbers on the following pages, as they have fully trained staff personal who really do care about you. I care about you too. Email me at roger@rndpublishing.com and we can enter into a discussion that can help ease the pain you're going through, because I've been there too.

I was rescued from myself by the grace and mercy of God, along with my loving, patient, and understanding wife at a time when I too, thought all hope was lost. I was so wrong and thank God every day for His intervention. Whether you're a believer or not, things will get better once you open up and share your struggle with others. It is so true, and I know right now it may be hard to envision that, but it's a fact. Dark times come and go, but the good times can and will more than outweigh those difficult, scary, and sad times.

• • •

My journey has been long, but by no means is it over. It could have been. Yours isn't over either. If you get anything from this short book, get this: When you think no one cares about you, you are making a huge mistake. God cares! I care, and others care, too. You just don't feel that right now, but you can and will. Don't struggle alone or in silence. You are worth more than that! There is a huge network of support out there, people who are dedicated to help you, but you have to take that first step to put away any preconceived notions that mental illness is shameful disease. It is not. If you are struggling, I pray you find the strength to open up about it and come forward. I just did.

Let hope and healing begin...

IMPORTANT HELP HOTLINE INFORMATION

NAMI (National Alliance on Mental Illness) National Helpline
800-950-6264 • www.nami.org

National Suicide Hotline
800-273-TALK (8255) • www.suicidepreventionlifeline.org

American Foundation for Suicide Prevention
Text TALK to: 741741 • 212-363-3500 • www.afsp.org

Veteran's Administration Suicide Hotline
Text: 838255 • 800-273-8255 • www.veteranscrisisline.net

Additional Mental Health Websites:

National Institute for Mental Health
www.nimh.nih.gov

Bring Change to Mind
www. BringChange2Mind.org

Mental Health First Aid
www.mentalhealthfirstaid.org